Poetic Pieces

P.B. McNally

Paper Doll

© P.B. McNally 1998

First Published in 1998 by
Paper Doll
Belasis Hall,
Coxwold Way,
Billingham,
Cleveland.

ISBN: 1 86248 034 6

Typeset by CBS, Felixstowe, Suffolk
Printed by Lintons Printers, Co. Durham

For Margaret, a true Christian

CONTENTS

Our Show	1
Bombed	2
Beverages	2
Today	3
Wishes	3
Abandoned Pets	4
Jungle Victors	5
House-Mouse	6
Pensioner Ponders	7
Fidelity	8
Tin Monster	8
Sing Song	9
Cricket, Lovely Cricket	10
Memories	11
Wedge Of Yellow	12
Wee Saga	13
Moving Fingers	13
Doubles	14
Them And Us	14
Spring	15
Sleeping Partner	15
Use Your Loaf	16
Taking Over	16
Home Bird	17
Where Will It End?	18
Fag End	19
Unhealthy Service	20
Urban Dawn	21

Wouldn't It Be . . . ?	22
On The Move	23
Afterthoughts (One)	24
Don't Go Yet	28
The Umpire	30
Solar Glare	32
Never Finished	32
Tee Up	33
Why Grumble?	33
Motive	34
The Inevitable End	35
Traffic Jam	36
Smile Your Way	37
Breathless Hush	38
Take Care	39
Ahoy, Tannoy	40
Virtue	40
Comparison	41
Everyone's A Person	42
Springtime	43
Weird Bird	44
Teamwork	44
Bookmaker	45
Global Madness	46
Rain	47
Serenity	48
Expensive Chuckies	48
You Can't Take It With You	49
Shadows	49
Ashes To Ashes	50
All Gone	51

Merry Father Christmas	51
Birth	52
Afterthoughts (Two)	53

OUR SHOW

A hardy annual is our show,
All the locals try to go.
Wives and hubbies in best togs,
Kids unlimited. Sorry, no dogs.
Rose and tulip colour the Hall,
Hard to see unless one is tall,
Lilies, begonias, hyacinths too,
Even bottles of home-made brew.
Gigantic peas burst their pods,
Prizes as usual for the same old bods,
Tall gladioli based in wood blocks,
Turn up pink noses at scented stocks.
Carpets of turf edged by thickets,
Hide stout ladies with raffle tickets,
Then it's tea and buns, out in the rain,
Back to the soil till it's Show Time again.

BOMBED

The plane flew so high in the sky
    That I gazed up by and by.
Why did that pigeon have to shy
    That unwanted gift in my eye?

BEVERAGES

Office staff often discuss
    The merits of their tea,
Wondering if it's cocoa,
    Coffee, or simply disagree.

TODAY

Ponder not on yesterday
    Which cannot be changed,
Think instead about today
    Which can be re-arranged.

WISHES

May your tears be few, joys galore,
May problems come in easy stages,
May love be yours forever more,
May all your jobs pay top wages.

ABANDONED PETS

Christmas is a time for joy,
    For every girl and boy
Yet, on Boxing Day, a lot
    Abandon poor Kit or Spot.

JUNGLE VICTORS

Solar glare dazzled dehydrated youth,
As he stood with hands shaking,
Trapped inside the barbed-wire coils,
Mistily squinting and inwardly quaking.

They came suddenly and aggressively,
Vociferous, pounding; wielding death,
Through dank, concealing undergrowth,
Framed by tall teak; exuding sour breath.

Waving long lethal swords; running;
Bespectacled, suicidal officers leading;
Life memory unwound before lad's eyes,
Swiftly; no inclination or time for reading.

He fired blindly, shakily, hopefully,
Sweating body heaving; mind upset;
Fighting for the folks back home,
Or so *They* said – with false regret.

Tracers flew, illuminating nightmare,
As darkness came and guns barked,
Limbless comrades lay pumping gore;
Enemy torsos, too, were not unmarked.

Upon looking back it all seems unreal,
Whys, wherefores; politician sinners,
Young lives – and years – lost forever,
Jackals and vultures the only winners.

HOUSE-MOUSE

Oh, tiny creature in the cellar,
Shy, elusive, frightened fella,
Scuttling away at slightest sound,
Into a dusty hole in the ground.

Creeping about at dead of night,
Nibbling anything edible in sight,
Take care though whatever you do,
'Cos our Tom Cat truly fancies you!

PENSIONER PONDERS

Standing there watching points,
Mind alert but creaking joints,
Smiling eyes, tolerant manner,
He muses about the demo banner.

NO MORE WARS – PEACE FOR ALL,
Tramping feet and parrot call,
DOWN WITH LAW – KILL ALL LEADERS,
Old man shouts: Silly Bleeders!

FIDELITY

Jones never chases after girls,
Not even those with auburn curls,
The reason why is plain to see,
Mrs Jones is much bigger than he.

TIN MONSTER

King Car is now a God
    To Modern Man is seems,
We now take second place
    To what Tin Monster deems.

SING SONG

Some folk sing in the bath
    Others hum in the loo,
Dogs bark in their kennels
    While pussy cats simply mew.

CRICKET, LOVELY CRICKET

Sodden turf and darkening skies,
White-clad men with anxious eyes,
Score board reading just two runs,
Ladies buttering some soggy buns.

Shivering fielders hop about,
Waiting for a chance to shout,
Frozen floozie crouched in chair,
Coldly ignores a masculine stare.

Ice Cream sales amount to nil,
Wind is howling down the hill,
Bringing rain in buckets plenty,
Stopping score from reaching twenty.

MEMORIES

Reverie-strolling on a misty day
    By vandalised tomb stones,
Passing names weather-worn away
    Over graves of rotting bones.

Meditating on moss-covered seat
    Near loved ones at rest,
Feeling neither cold or heat
    To hold a personal inquest.

Then, coming home through traffic roar
    To a lonely flat so cheerless,
Uncaring of ambition any more;
    Tormented by memories so peerless.

Sleep comes slowly, then I dream
    Of happy days; an ever-open door,
And wake alone outside life's stream,
    Waiting to join those gone before.

WEDGE OF YELLOW

Wedge of yellow hanging there,
Dried-up, dusty, rocky, bare,
Then man came in rocket ship,
Your ancient secrets to strip.

He robbed you of most mystery,
Should really have let it be,
There's reason in 'most everything,
Yet you have no birds to sing.

And nothing growing or to drink,
No benches for to sit and think,
Or a slice of promised cheese,
Nor a gentle murmuring breeze.

Surely there is some good in you,
Go on, moon, please give us a clue,
Do you provide a last resting place,
For lost souls which leaves no trace?

WEE SAGA

I wonder why, as a woodland tree,
All local dogs have to pick on me?

MOVING FINGERS

As fingers on the ward clock move around,
I wonder if it is to Hell that I am bound.

DOUBLES

Two heads are better than one, they say,
But at the cinema there's double to pay.

THEM AND US

Some folks have more than two houses,
Others live rough with ragged trousers.

SPRING

Spring is such a bracing time,
    Filled with love and roses,
That's the theory, we are told,
    But all one sees is runny noses.

SLEEPING PARTNER

Boxing is a manly sport,
    Full of pain and gore,
Except for the manager,
    Who's never hurt – or poor.

USE YOUR LOAF

The secret of having a fling,
    Frowned on by those without,
Is covering tracks so subtle,
    That one is never found out.

TAKING OVER

Soccer's not for men alone,
    Females, too, can score,
Dashing all the way to goal,
    Looking, sadly, undemure.

HOME BIRD

Heading for the City
In a crowded train,
Deserving every pity
Under mounting strain,
Think of lucky Rosie
Changing baby's bib,
All warm and cosy –
    To hell with Women's Lib.

WHERE WILL IT END?

Our freezer sure holds naught,
    For many items can not be bought,
And mounting debts make us cry,
    As we strive to beat the other guy.

We have colour telly; an extra room,
    Georgian windows; a smell of doom,
With new bills coming every week,
    As the Jones's title we vainly seek.

FAG END

What good will it do you,
    Hanging there, burning away,
        In yellow-stained lips, pray?

Filling lungs with lethal tar,
    All for what, you fool?
        Obstinate as a mule.

Do you enjoy dying, slowly,
    In pain, coughing and wheezing,
        Like your throat needs greasing?

Give it up, drugged human,
    Why pay to suffer, stupid you,
        With your health – and money, too?

UNHEALTHY SERVICE

The NHS is just a football,
Kicked around by one and all,
Meanwhile, old and infirm wait,
For operations that come too late.

URBAN DAWN

It is five in the morning,
There is no need for a light
With air fresh and fragrant,
And the sky clear and bright.

So dress, wash and leave the house,
And tip-toe quietly like a mouse,
To savour now the unspoiled air,
Then breathe in deeply without a care.

Stretch your legs, swing your arms,
Enjoy fully these heavenly charms,
Because four hours later it's no joke,
You'll be inhaling fumy smoke.

WOULDN'T IT BE . . . ?

Wouldn't it be smashing
If errors were forgiven
– Without a verbal lashing?

Wouldn't it be sweet
If smiles replaced frowns
– As folk pass in the street?

Wouldn't it be great
If deprived came first
– And all had a full plate?

Wouldn't it be grand
If life was a ball
– Truly enjoyed by all?

ON THE MOVE

Today's the day, the last one here,
Our plans complete, the time is near,
Spot barks excitedly at all the fuss,
The kids are banished on to the bus.

Mum and Dad look so lost and sad,
Remember good times, not the bad,
Feeling tired with all the packing,
Then undoing the carpet tacking.

The van arrives with aproned men,
First they clear our Father's den,
Neighbours call amid the bustle,
Some do cry, paper hankies rustle.

Our new home looks grubby and small,
Spot prowls around smelling the hall,
Kids sit tensed, so strangely quiet,
Dad's all edgy, Mum's hair is a sight.

AFTERTHOUGHTS (ONE)

ROOFLESS

There was a young fellow from Kent,
Who could not pay his rent,
    So he went to the bank,
    Where his hopes sank,
And now he lives in a tent.

PENNILESS

There was an old man from Stoke
Who bought a pig in a poke,
    But when he got home,
    In the poke was a gnome,
So now he's completely broke.

GRACE

We thank Thee, Lord, for this tasty repast,
And sincerely trust that it won't be the last.

JAILBIRD

There was a young lady from Manila,
Who was fond of ice cream vanilla,
    But when she ran out of cash,
    Robbing a bank was so rash,
Now she eats porridge to fill her.

GARDEN BLUES

The flowers sure look great,
Right up to the garden gate,
The lawn is lush up to the tree,
But my poor back is killing me!

POLICY

Insurance firms state as their aim,
    To cover all misfortune for you,
But when you dare put in a claim,
    You're told: Get in the queue.

DON'T GO YET

Don't go yet
    Wait for tomorrow,
I'm not conditioned
    For instant sorrow.

Give me space,
    Time to breathe,
Linger awhile, dear,
    Before you leave.

The doctors confirmed
    What I thought,
They, too, rate your
    Chances as naught.

Hope still flickers
    In my heart,
I'm not willing
    We should part.

You lie quiet
    So deathly pale,
Not quite beyond
    That eternal veil.

I sit tensed
    Praying and hoping,
Trying to look
    Composed, not moping.

Ward chatter irks
    Patients tease nurses,
Man from operation
    Rants and curses.

Life should remain
    In suspended animation,
All should join
    In my meditation.

Your eyes open,
    Look past mine,
Close again slowly
    Without a sign.

Don't die now
    Stay with me,
I'll wait forever
    If need be.

THE UMPIRE

Proudly he stood erect by the wicket,
Seemingly always looking at his ease,
Ignoring all jeers from the thicket,
Or watching girls laying out teas.

He tossed pebbles around his pocket,
With one eye kept firm on the light,
Dissenting batsmen soon got a rocket,
His hand signal was a bowler's delight.

He walked briskly to work all the week,
As foreman he maintained strict control,
But to the manager he was ever so meek,
And, aged fifty, he signed on the dole.

There were no favours for the home club,
They were aware of that only too well,
So no-one paid for his favourite grub,
Or dare buy him a pint at the Bell.

He once did play for the home team,
A moderate sort of bowler, they say,
Being fairly good at using the seam,
His long hops were slogged far away.

His batting was reckoned not a lot,
Four runs snicked off the bat's edge,
Was the highest score he ever got,
And the ball was lost in a hedge.

He was used as a scorer from then,
But not when they played the best,
He was too slow counting after ten,
So they made him take a long rest.

He knows his eyes they are failing,
And his thoughts are sometimes remote,
So he dozes alone by the park railing,
Day-dreaming of when he wore a white coat.

SOLAR GLARE

The sun comes up, the sun goes down,
Lights up the village and the town,
Roasts all the bathers on the beach,
Pushes up the price of a mouldy peach.

NEVER FINISHED

Making beds and washing up,
Cleaning, dusting, cooking,
Polishing your life away –
All while no one's looking.

TEE UP

Golf is a peculiar game
    Completely Greek to me,
First you find a caddie,
    Then off you go to tee.

WHY GRUMBLE?

I wonder why folk grumble
    At each and every tumble,
When they know full well
    Life can never truly gel?

MOTIVE

Work for some is all honey,
    Others labour just for love;
Another motive is mere money,
    But *my* wife gives *me* a shove.

THE INEVITABLE END

There is no end to the tiresome chase,
Of us searching for a parking place,
And things get worse as cars multiply,
Our only option soon will be to fly.

Surely there is one inevitable end,
Before we all end up around the bend,
The numbers of cars will have to drop,
Else all traffic will permanently stop.

TRAFFIC JAM

It's hard to find a space to stay,
Even if you've the money to pay,
For Wardens haunt most every street,
Aided by police-persons on the beat.

So round and round you must go,
Perhaps break down, need a tow,
And even to pause on yellow lines,
Makes you liable for usual fines.

SMILE YOUR WAY

No matter how bad your day,
    Hide it all behind a smile;
Ignore all wounding words,
    Happy faces soon beguile.

Dismiss grey skies and rain,
    Laugh away the gloomy news;
Infect people with your joy,
    And banish all those blues.

BREATHLESS HUSH

There's a breathless hush in the ward tonight,
With not a bedpan or bottle in sight,
As most of the patients lie uncannily still,
All sleeping soundly – with the aid of a pill.

Porters and visitors have long been banished,
The tactful Auxiliary has merely vanished,
And Sister looks lovely – really great,
Waiting for the Registrar – her favourite date.

TAKE CARE

When life proceeds trouble free,
Please take a tip from wary me,
Stop right now from getting bolder,
And take a look over your shoulder.

The day is bright, you feel grand,
So stay alert for that Evil Hand,
Instigating problems by the score,
Followed by accidents more and more.

All it needs is a fly in the eye,
To turn joy into a martyr's cry,
Or some vexed words from a friend,
To rapidly alter a cheery trend.

Remain on guard when all seems right,
There is no warning of sudden blight,
Life is never all milk and honey,
Even wise men can lose their money.

AHOY, TANNOY

Heard above machine roar,
    Comes a ghastly sound,
Something from the Top Ten,
    I will bet you a pound.

VIRTUE

There's no virtue in
    Helping one's own kin,
Or anyone well adored
    If folk abhorred are ignored.

COMPARISON

Any pet like a dog or a cat,
    Living in Britain pleasant,
Is treated much better,
    Than an African peasant.

EVERYONE'S A PERSON

That bundle of rags
Wrapped in old bags
And round the bend
Is still a friend,
    'Cos everyone's a person.

Old Meg who stinks
Mad Fred who drinks
Should not be ignored
If never adored,
    'Cos everyone's a person.

God made us all;
Short, fat or tall,
Po-faced or cute,
Polite or a brute,
    'Cos everyone's a person.

The one we hate
Becomes our mate
If we free our minds
And accept all kinds,
    'Cos everyone's a person.

SPRINGTIME

New leaves and buds joyfully appear,
Stimulating vigour for another year,
Hearts beat faster, thoughts do wing,
Heady vibrations announce it's Spring.

A glance, a smile, or just a word,
Make one feel as light as a bird,
All is heavenly – except the weather,
Nothing matters – only being together.

A look, a letter, or a phone call,
Changes the humdrum into a ball,
Timorous, rapturous, holding hands,
Turns drab streets into golden sands.

Thoughts of dull environment distraction,
Are soon diverted by a mutual attraction,
Feelings outstrip all the material plans,
Except, perhaps, for the calling of banns.

WEIRD BIRD

There's a weird kind of bird,
    Who seems to fancy me,
As lying wounded my eyes meet,
    Those of a vulture in a tree.

TEAMWORK

Managers, workers and plant,
    Together make up a team,
They truly need each other,
    More than it might seem.

BOOKMAKER

He has such a wondrous time,
    Laughing behind a partition,
Watching punters eagerly ensure,
    He suffers not from malnutrition.

GLOBAL MADNESS

Uncaring people pollute water, seed
    and feed,
Turning earth into moon dust for power
    and greed.

The air we breathe, deteriorates,
    and, for men,
Risks abnormality – for them
    and children.

Some folk fight on without stealth
    and risk health,
Against Press tycoon ridicule,
    and industrial wealth.

The time has come, some believe,
    and sanction,
The ousting of material faction,
    and taking action,
To stop this suicidal madness
    and global destruction.

RAIN

Dark clouds race across the sky,
    Breezes quicken, rain is nigh,
Leaves and paper blow about,
    Scared children run and shout.

Chilling wind cools the air,
    Flapping awnings start to tear,
Sheets of water cut off sight,
    Drivers pray for a guiding light.

Faces press against window panes,
    Farmers cheer down country lanes,
Housewives groan at washing wet,
    Punters moan; they can't have a bet.

It pleases some; angers the rest,
    Gives river banks a severe test,
But without it, where would we be?
    Why, under the ground, you and me.

SERENITY

Sunshine, calm seas and blue skies,
A touch of heaven that God supplies.

EXPENSIVE CHUCKIES

Easter eggs are eggseedingly nice,
If you can shell out the price.

YOU CAN'T TAKE IT WITH YOU

What's the point in leaving a million,
If one is destined for naked oblivion?

SHADOWS

Holiday planning brightens a dark day,
Actuality is sometimes dull and grey.

ASHES TO ASHES

HE looks down in deep sorrow,
Planning for a new tomorrow,
Regretful now of man's free will,
And his insane urge to kill.

People care for cars and drink,
Of sick and poor they don't think,
There seems no end to earthly wars,
It's hard to find a genuine cause.

Sleep around; blaspheme a lot,
Alcoholics Unlimited; legal Pot,
Excessive sex; no wedding rings,
Okay for all, the Pop star sings.

Religious strife splits nations,
Even separates family relations,
Yet of one thing there is a must,
We all finish up as polluted dust.

ALL GONE

When we depart this earthly place,
Of us there will soon be no trace.

MERRY FATHER CHRISTMAS

Santa comes every year
    To our happy home,
Full of love and cheer
    Looking like a gnome.

Swaying up the stairs
    Bobble hat askew,
Whiskers need repairs
    While Dad sups his Home Brew.

BIRTH

A young wife stirred in the night,
Pain-racked, she cried with fright,
Husband dressed and quickly ran,
Returning soon with a medical man,
Next a wrinkled face appeared,
Red raw, until lungs were cleared.

Oh, helpless bundle lying there,
So newly-born and needing care,
Innocence radiates cherub face,
Angelic, pure and full of grace,
Conceived by a couple happy,
Contented even to change a nappy!

AFTERTHOUGHTS (TWO)

COUCH POTATO

Supping beer while watching telly,
Brings on a coronary and a fat belly.

EPITAPH ONE

Poor old Ben has popped his clogs,
He died a pauper from backing dogs.

EPITAPH TWO

Charlie supped gallons of frothy beer,
Now he's laid out on a flowery bier.

EARLY DEPARTURE

Please take me, Lord, early in the day,
    Before I speak or revel,
'Cos if I'm left to do it my way,
    I'll surely join the devil.

WANDERING THOUGHTS

I try to pray most every day,
    But my thoughts ever wander,
I think of all those bills to pay,
    And on my shopping ponder.

MIRACLE WANTED

Dear Lord, we need your aid,
To supply a miracle dinner,
'Cos all our bills are unpaid,
And none of us can get much thinner.